The month of March, from the illuminated manuscript *Les Trés Riches Heures du duc de Berry*

The Story of a Special Day
Volume 90

March

30

89th day of the year
(90th in leap years)
276 days remaining
until the end of the year.

by Michael Dobson

Timespinner
Press

Table of Contents

Cover: Detail from *Irises*, by Vincent Van Gogh — for the Event of the Day.

Seán O'Casey, by Reginald V. Gray

March 30 Quotations

"Wouldn't it be terrible if you'd spent all your life doing everything you were supposed to do, didn't drink, didn't smoke, didn't eat things, took lots of exercise, all the things you didn't want to do, and suddenly one day you were run over by a big red bus, and as the wheels were crunching into you you'd say 'Oh my god, I could have got so drunk last night!' That's the way you should live your life, as if tomorrow you'll be run over by a big red bus."

Queen Elizabeth, the Queen Mother, died March 30, 2002

"I hope you're all Republicans."

Ronald Reagan, US President, to his doctors and nurses following the assassination attempt on March 30, 1981

"A man should always be drunk, Minnie, when he talks politics — it's the only way in which to make them important."

Seán O'Casey, playwright, born March 30, 1880

"The more I think about it, the more I feel that there is nothing more truly artistic than to love people."

Vincent van Gogh, painter, born March 30, 1853

Self-Portrait (1889), Vincent Van Gogh

Event of the Day
Vincent Van Gogh Born

One of the most influential and important painters of modern times, Vincent Willem van Gogh (March 30, 1853 – July 29, 1880) spent his life in obscurity and poverty. Although he created over 2,100 works of art in an active career that lasted a mere decade, he sold only a single painting in his lifetime.

Van Gogh was born in the Netherlands province of North Brabant, and was sent away to boarding school at the age of 11. He learned to draw there, but dropped out after a year to return home. At the age of 16, he went to work for an art dealer in The Hague, and was later transferred to the London office. He was initially successful, but after a transfer to Paris he became increasingly resentful of the way art was treated, which led to his termination. He worked a series of odd jobs, including school teacher, minister's assistant, and bookstore clerk, before deciding he wanted to become a pastor like his father. This didn't work out either. He failed his entrance exam to the school of theology and failed a three-month course to become a missionary. In spite of that, he took a post as a missionary in Belgium, where he slept on straw to be more like those to whom he was ministering. This upset the local church authorities, who fired him yet again for "undermining the dignity of the priesthood."

Van Gogh returned home to the increasing consternation and concern of his parents. By now his mental illness had reached a state that led his father to look into having his son committed to a lunatic asylum. Then his brother Theo intervened, suggesting that Vincent pursue art more seriously.

Vincent Van Gogh was in his mid-twenties when he enrolled at the Académie Royale des Beaux-Arts in Brussels. After a year studying anatomy, modeling, and perspective, he moved back with his parents and continued drawing. He proposed to his widowed cousin, seven years his senior, but she refused emphatically: *"Nooit, neen, nimmer!"* ("No, nay, never!"). Moving again to The Hague, he studied painting with a cousin-in-law, the Dutch realist painter Anton Mauve and began a relationship with an alcoholic prostitute named Sien, who had a boy who may or may not have been Van Gogh's. (Yielding to parental pressure, he broke off the relationship and refused to acknowledge the child; Sien drowned herself some years later.

Van Gogh's first major work, *The Potato Eaters*, was painted in 1885, and for the first time elements of the art world began to take a small interest in him. His work was first exhibited in the window of a paint dealer in The Hague. Over the next two years, he would complete nearly 200 paintings, characterized by dark brown earth tones rather than the vibrant colors that would distinguish his greatest work. Living in a small room in Antwerp, he ate poorly and began to drink absinthe, all the while continuing to paint even with worsening health.

In 1886, he moved to Paris to live with his brother Theo, now an art dealer, who found the living arrangement "almost unbearable" and terminated the arrangement the following year.

The Potato Eaters (1885), Vincent Van Gogh

Exposed to the Impressionists in Paris, Van Gogh's paintings began to use brighter colors and bolder paint strokes, becoming more representative of the artist he would become. Well known works of this period include *Portrait of Père Tanguy* and *Bridges Across the Seine at Asnieres*. He began to meet other artists, including Paul Gauguin, Toulouse-Lautrec, and Georges Seurat. However, life in the city began to wear on him, and in 1888 he moved again, this time to Arles, in the south of France.

It was in Arles that Van Gogh's talent reached its zenith. While there, he would paint such masterpieces as *Bedroom in Arles, Still Life: Vase with Twelve Sunflowers, The Night Café,* and *Starry Night Over the Rhone* (an early version of the better known *The Starry Night*). A visit from Paul Gauguin in 1888 led to the two men becoming estranged. Van Gogh threatened Gauguin with a razor blade, but panicked and fled to a brothel he frequently visited. While there, he cut off part of his left ear (the earlobe and a bit more, not the whole ear as is often believed), wrapped it in newspaper, and presented it to one of the prostitutes. Later, Gauguin and the police found Van Gogh unconscious in his home, covered in blood.

Van Gogh's mental health became increasingly precarious. He experienced hallucinations and was convinced he was being poisoned. In May 1889, he committed himself to a mental hospital about twenty miles away. His brother Theo arranged for him to have two rooms, adjoining cells with barred windows, so he would have a studio.

While in the clinic, he painted *The Starry Night, The Sower, Two Peasant Women Digging in a Snow-Covered Field at Sunset,* and *Sorrowing Old Man.* He became noticed in the Paris art world, with one reviewer describing him as "a genius," and he was invited to participate in the annual exhibition of avant-garde painters in Brussels.

On the verge of success and recognition, Van Gogh left the clinic to be treated by Dr. Paul Gachet , who had treated other artists. In seventy days, he created seventy paintings, including *Wheat Field With Crows*, *Portrait of Dr. Gachet*, and what is considered to be his final work, *Daubigny's Garden*. But beginning in February 1890, he slipped into a terrible depression, punctuated by periods of hallucination.

On July 27, 1890, at the age of 37, Van Gogh apparently shot himself, although the gun was never found. He walked back to his apartment, where he was seen by two doctors, neither of them surgeons. They bandaged him up and left him alone in his room, smoking a pipe. He was still alive the next day, when his brother Theo arrived, but died that evening. According to his brother, Van Gogh's last words were, "The sadness will last forever."

Van Gogh's fame, which was just beginning to grow at the time of his death, continued steadily. Major exhibitions of his work appeared in Paris, Cologne, New York, and Berlin in the first years of the twentieth century, and by mid-century, he was generally considered one of the greatest painters in history. His works are among the most expensive paintings ever sold, with three of them changing hands for more than $100 million.

The nature of his mental illness continues to be debated, with over thirty different diagnoses suggested. Whatever the cause, malnutrition and absinthe clearly played a role. His influence, however, was vast.

He has been called the "trailblazer of modern art," and elements of his style can be seen in the works of Willem de Kooning, Jackson Pollock, and many others. The Van Gogh Museum in Amsterdam is the most visited museum in the Netherlands, with nearly 1.5 million visitors in 2012.

How do you pronounce his last name? While most English speakers say (incorrectly), "van GOH," (-oh as in no), native Dutch speakers would say "vun (or fun) KHOKH," (-v as in vet or –f as in fit, -u as in bun, -o as in oh, and -kh as in Scottish "loch." For English speakers, we turned to the BBC Pronunciation Unit, which recommends "van GOKH" (-v as in vet, -g as in get, -o as in oh, and –kh as in loch), a pronunciation also found in various dictionaries.

The Starry Night (1885), Vincent Van Gogh

March 30 Holidays and Celebrations

National Doctor's Day (United States)

National Doctor's Day, celebrated each March 30 in the United States, commemorates the first use of anesthesia for surgery, by Dr. Crawford Long on March 30, 1842.

Doctor's Day is celebrated in other countries on different dates.Cuba recognizes December 3 as the birthday of pioneering yellow fever researcher Carlos Juan Finley. Iran commemorates the birth of Avicenna (ابن سينا), author of some 40 books on medicine, on August 23 (Shahrivar 1). India honors physician Dr. Bidhan Chandra Roy, born July 1, 1882.

Spiritual Baptist/Shouter Liberation Day (Trinidad and Tobago)

The Spiritual Baptist faith, also known as Shouter Baptist, originated with former American slaves who fought for the British as the Corps of Colonial Marines in the War of 1812, and were subsequently settled in Trinidad. Mixing Christianity with elements of traditional African religion, the Spiritual Baptists were nicknamed "Shouters" by the British because of their open-air religious celebrations.

In 1917, Trinidad and Tobago passed the Shouter Prohibition Ordinance. On March 30, 1951, the ordinance was repealed, and in 1996, the Government of Trinidad and Tobago declared a public holiday celebrating the repeal.

Yom al-Ard (Land Day) (Palestinian Territory and Palestinian Diaspora)

Palestinians commemorate March 30 as Yom al-Ard (Land Day, يوم الأرض). In 1976, following an Israeli government plan to expropriate land for security and settlement purposes, Palestinians and Israeli Arabs organized a general strike and marches, which resulted in violent confrontations with Israeli military and police. Annual strikes and protests have taken place each year since then.

National Turkey Neck Soup Day (United States)

In the United States, almost every day of the year is dedicated to a particular food. Sponsored by manufacturers, retailers, farmers, or simply fans, these days are often proclaimed by the President, Congress, state governors, or mayors.

March 30 is National Turkey Neck Soup Day. While you might expect this special day to follow Thanksgiving, perhaps it is there to remind us that turkeys can be eaten year round. Although turkey necks are mostly bone, they do make an excellent soup broth — though you'll need to add a lot of vegetables.

Christian Feast Days

In *Western Christianity*, saints commemorated on March 30 include Blessed Amadeus IX of Savoy, John Climacus, Mamertinus of Auxerre, Quirinus of Neuss, and Tola of Clonard.

In *Eastern Orthodox Christianity*, it is the commemoration of the prophets Joad and Joel; the holy apostles Sosthenes, Apollos, Cephas, Caesar, and Epaphroditus; Saint Eubula; John the Hermit of Cicilia; and Saint Sophronius. It is also the translation of the relicts of the Martyr-King Edmund of East Anglia and the Repose of Blessed Matrona (Mynikova) the Barefoot of St. Petersburg. (These are celebrated on April 12 by "Old Calendarists.")

Other Holidays (United States unless otherwise noted)

Some holidays are simply made up by individuals, companies, or other organizations, and whether they become widely adopted depends on whether people choose to celebrate them. Here are some opportunities to celebrate on March 30.

March 30 is I Am In Control Day (commemorating Secretary of State Alexander Haig's declaration following the 1981 assassination attempt on President Ronald Reagan), Take a Walk in the Park Day, The Grass is Always Browner on the Other Side of the Fence Day (to inspire people to be happy with what they have), and Pencil Day (on March 30, 1958, Hyman Lipman received a patent for a pencil with an attached eraser).

US President Ronald Reagan (center) waves outside the Washington Hilton Hotel just before he is shot, March 30, 1981.

From left to right: Unknown man (in pinstripe suit), Secret Service agent Jerry Parr (in raincoat), Press Secretary James Brady (wounded), unknown military officer, Ronald Reagan, Reagan aide Michael Deaver, an unidentified policeman, Officer Thomas Delahanty (with hands in pockets, wounded), and Secret Service agent Tim McCarthy (in light blue suit, wounded).

What Happened on March 30?

1814 – Battle of Paris

The War of the Sixth Coalition between Napoleon Bonaparte's French Empire and an alliance of Russia, Austria, and Prussia, began in the aftermath of Napoleon's failed invasion of Russia. The culminating act, the Battle of Paris, took place on March 30-31, 1814, pitting a Coalition army of about 150,000 against 50,000 French soldiers commanded by Napoleon's brother Joseph. The Coalition victory resulted in Napoleon's forced abdication and exile to the island of Elba.

1822 – Florida Territory Formed

In response to escaped slaves fleeing to Spanish-ruled La Florida, American forces led by General (later President) Andrew Jackson invaded in 1818 and forced the Spanish to negotiate a treaty that surrendered La Florida to the United States. On March 30, 1822, the newly-acquired territory was incorporated as the Territory of Florida. Florida became the 27th state admitted to the Union on March 3, 1845.

1842 – Ether Anesthesia First Used in Surgery

While the use of various substances for anesthesia dates back before recorded history, the compounds were unreliable, toxic, or addictive. Diethyl ether, along with nitrous oxide, were two of the first modern anesthestics, notable because of the greater gap between a medically useful dosage and a toxic overdose.

The first use of ether as an anesthetic in surgery took place on March 30, 1842, when Georgia physician Dr. Crawford Long used it in a surgery to remove a tumor from the neck of a patient. The Crawford W. Long Museum in Jefferson, Georgia, commemorates his achievement, and Long was featured on a postage stamp in 1940. National Doctor's Day in the US is celebrated on March 30 to mark Dr. Long's achievement.

1856 – End of the Crimean War

On March 30, 1856, the Treaty of Paris, between Russia and an alliance of the British, French, Sardinians, and Ottomans, was signed, bringing the Crimean War to a close. The Crimean War, which lasted approximately 18 months, is considered the first modern war, but it is best remembered today for the nursing practices of Florence Nightingale and the Charge of the Light Brigade.

Dr. Crawford W. Long

1867 – Alaska Purchase

Fearing that the British would seize what was then known as Russian America in a war, the Russian Empire decided instead to sell their North American holdings to the United States. Negotiations took place between the Russian minister to the United States, Eduard de Stoeckl (Эдуард Стекль), and the US Secretary of State, William Seward. Although the final purchase price of $7.2 million worked out to about 2¢ an acre, public opinion was mixed on the acquisition, and the deal became known as "Seward's Folly," an opinion that changed only when the Klondike Gold Rush began in 1896.

A US Treasury check for $7.2 million, used to purchase
Alaska from Russia, March 30, 1867

1909 – Queensboro Bridge Opens

On March 30, 1909, the Queensboro Bridge linking Manhattan to Long Island City opened to traffic, at a cost of $18 million and 50 lives.

Known as the Blackwell's Island Bridge and the 59th Street Bridge (immortalized in the Simon & Garfunkel hit "The 59th Street Bridge Song (Feelin' Groovy),") it was renamed the Ed Koch Queensboro Bridge in honor of the New York City mayor in 2010. The bridge has made numerous appearances in television shows and movies, including the credits for the TV shows *Archie Bunker's Place, The King of Queens, Taxi, Rescue Me,* and *Alphas,* and the poster for Woody Allen's 1979 film *Manhattan.*

Queensboro Bridge (Blackwell's Island Bridge), 1910

1964 – *Jeopardy* Premiers

Known as "the thinking man's game show," *Jeopardy* premiered on television March 30, 1964, with original host Art Fleming.

In *Jeopardy*, contestants win cash by giving the correct question ("What is Florida?") in response to an answer ("The 27th US State.") In 1984, the show returned with new host Alex Trebek.

1981 – Attempted Assassination of President Ronald Reagan

On Monday, March 30, 1981, US President Ronald Reagan and three others were shot by John Hinckley, Jr., as they left a speaking engagement at the Washington Hilton Hotel. Reagan suffered a cracked rib and a punctured lung, but recovered fully, becoming the first serving US President to survive being shot in an assassination attempt.

Of the other victims, Press Secretary James Brady was paralyzed, DC police officer Thomas Delahanty suffered permanent nerve damage and was forced to retire, and Secret Service agent Tim McCarthy, who shielded Reagan with his body, was shot in the abdomen but recovered fully.

The shooter, John Hinckley, Jr., who was apparently motivated by an obsession with actress Jodie Foster, was found not guilty by reason of insanity and committed to St. Elizabeth's Hospital in DC, where he remains at the time of this writing.

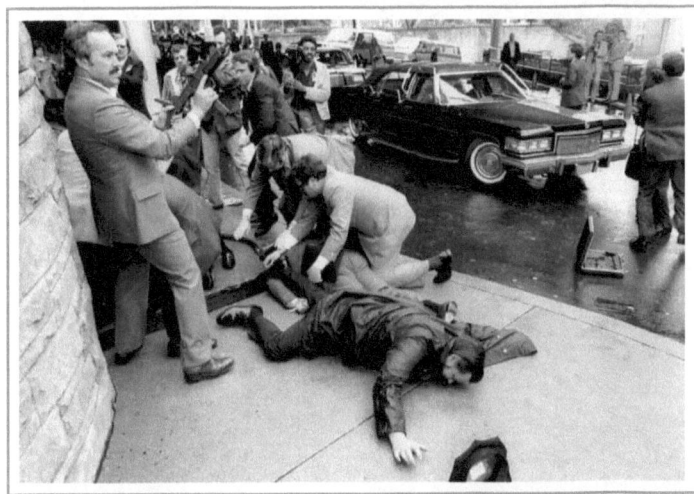

Immediately following the assassination attempt on Ronald Reagan: Officer Thomas Delahanty (foreground) and Press Secretary James Brady lie wounded as an unidentified Secret Service agent stands guard.

Self-Portrait at 69 Years, Francisco Goya

Who Was Born on March 30?

Art and Illustration

Marc Davis (March 30, 1913 – January 12, 2000)

Artist and animator Marc Davis was one of Walt Disney Studios core animators, referred to as the "Nine Old Men." He designed and animated such characters as Cinderella, Tinker Bell, and Cruella De Vil, and created characters for Disney theme park attractions including "It's a Small World," "Pirates of the Caribbean," and "The Haunted Mansion."

Francisco Goya (March 30, 1746 – April 16, 1828)

Spanish painter and printmaker Francisco Goya (left) is considered by art critics to be both the last of the Old Masters and the first of the moderns. He is known for his many portraits; his print series about the Peninsular War, *Desastres de la Guerra (The Disasters of War)*; the paintings *La maja desnuda (The Nude Maja)* and *La maja vestida (The Clothed Maja)*; and his *Black Paintings,* including *Saturno devorando a su hijo (Saturn Devours His Son)*.

Business

Ingvar Kamprad (March 30, 1926 –)

Swedish businessman Ingvar Kamprad founded IKEA.

Crime and Punishment

Albert Pierrepoint (March 30, 1905 – July 10, 1992)

English hangman Albert Pierrepont executed over 400 people, about half of them war criminals, both in Great Britain and in Germany. The 2005 film *Pierrepoint* tells a somewhat fictionalized verion of his story.

Government and Military

McGeorge Bundy (March 30, 1919 – September 16, 1996)

McGeorge Bundy was National Security Advisor to US Presidents John F. Kennedy and Lyndon Johnson, and played a role in escalating US involvement in Vietnam. Following his government service, he was president of the Ford Foundation, and was included on Richard Nixon's "enemies list."

Richard Helms (March 30, 1913 – October 23, 2002)

Richard Helms served as Director of Central Intelligence (DCI) for US Presidents Lyndon Johnson and Richard Nixon. In 1977, while serving as US Ambassador to Iran, he became the only DCI convicted of misleading Congress, for his role in CIA operations in Chile. He received a two-year suspended sentence and a $2,000 fine after pleading nolo contendere to a misdemeanor offense. In 1983, President Ronald Reagan awarded Helms the National Security Medal and appointed him to a Presidential commission on national security.

Franz Oppenheimer (March 30, 1864 – September 30, 1943)

German-Jewish sociologist and political economist Franz Oppenheimer is best known for his 1908 book Der Staat (The State), a highly influential work on the origins and transformation of government institutions.

Mehmed the Conqueror (محمد ثانی) (March 30, 1432 – May 3, 1481)

Ottoman Sultan Mehmed II conquered Constantinople at the age of 21, ending the Byzantine Empire and replacing it with the Ottoman Empire, which would last six centuries as one of the world's most powerful states, until finally collapsing at the end of World War I.

He continued to rule for 31 years, expanding the empire into the Balkans and throughout Asia Minor.

Mehmed II enters Constantinople, Fausto Zonaro

Music

Norah Jones (March 30, 1979 –)

Singer-songwriter Geetali Norah Jones Shankar received five Grammy awards for her 2002 album *Come Away With Me*, which sold over 26 million copies, and went on to record several other platinum albums. She is the daughter of sitar virtuoso Ravi Shankar.

Céline Dion (March 30, 1968 –)

Canadian singer Céline Dion was named the best-selling female artist of all time in 2004, with sales exceeding 220 million albums worldwide. She has won five Grammy Awards, including Album of the Year and Record of the Year for "My Heart Will Go On (Love Theme from *Titanic*)."

Tracy Chapman (March 30, 1964 –)

American singer-songwriter Tracy Chapman (right, photo by Hans Hillewaert) has won four Grammy awards and has multi-platinum albums including her debut album, *Tracy Chapman*, and 1995's *New Beginning*. She is also known for her social activism.

M. C. Hammer (March 30, 1962 –)

Under his stage name M. C. Hammer (later just Hammer), rapper and dancer Stanley Kirk Burrell had major hits with 1990's "U Can't Touch This" and 1991's "2 Legit 2 Quit."

Eric Clapton (March 30, 1945 –)

Legendary guitarist, singer, and songwriter Eric Clapton is a three-time inductee into the Rock and Roll Hall of Fame, for his solo work and as a member of The Yardbirds and Cream. He is ranked second in Rolling Stone magazine's 100 Greatest Guitarists of All Time. His hits include "I Shot the Sheriff," "Layla," and "Tears in Heaven." He has received 17 Grammy awards.

Eric Clapton (Photo: F. Antolín Hernandez)

Graeme Edge (March 30, 1941 –)

Drummer and songwriter Graeme Edge is best known for his work with The Moody Blues, and (as of this writing) is the only remaining original member still performing in the band.

Astrud Gilberto (March 30, 1940 –)

Brazilian singer Astrud Gilberto is best known to North American audiences for her 1965 Grammy-winning hit "The Girl from Ipanema."

Frankie Laine (March 30, 1913 – February 6, 2007)

Singer and songwriter Frankie Laine's many hits include "Mule Train," "That Lucky Old Sun," "Jezebel," "Cool Water," and "Rawhide." While his career spanned everything from big band to rock, folk, jazz, and blues, he was best known for singing theme songs for many movie and television soundtracks, including *Gunfight at the O. K. Corral* and *Blazing Saddles*. He was nicknamed "Mr. Rhythm," "Old Leather Lungs," and "Mr. Steel Tonsils."

Ted Heath (March 30, 1902 – November 18, 1969)

Trombonist Ted Heath founded the most famous and successful British post-war big band, recording over 100 albums that sold over 20 million copies.

John Stafford Smith (March 30, 1750 – September 21, 1836)

British composer and musicologist John Stafford Smith is best known for writing the melody for "The Anacreontic Song" (also known as "To Anacreon in Heaven,") the official song of the Anacreontic Society, an 18th century London club of amateur musicians. Later, Francis Scott Key set his 1814 poem "Defence of Fort McHenry" to the same melody, and renamed it "The Star-Spangled Banner," which became the US national anthem.

Performing Arts

Jason Dohring (March 30, 1982 –)

Jason Dohring played Logan Echolls on the TV series *Veronica Mars* and co-starred in *Moonlight*.

Donna D'Errico (March 30, 1968 –)

Former *Playboy* Playmate Donna D'Errico had a starring role on the TV series *Baywatch* from 1996 to 1998.

Ian Ziering (March 30, 1964 –)

Ian Ziering is best known for his role as Steve Sanders on the TV series *Beverly Hills, 90210*.

Paul Reiser (March 30, 1957 –)

Comedian Paul Reiser is best known for his role in the 1990s sitcom *Mad About You*. His other work includes roles in *Diner* (1982), *Beverly Hills Cop* (1984) and its 1987 sequel, and *Aliens* (1986).

Robbie Coltrane (March 30, 1950 –)

Scottish actor Robbie Coltrane is best known for his role as Hogwarts gamekeeper Rubeus Hagrid in the *Harry Potter* films. He also played an ex-KGB officer in the James Bond film *GoldenEye* and *The World Is Not Enough*, and criminal psychologist "Fitz" Fitzgerald in the British crime drama *Cracker*.

Ray Magliozzi (March 30, 1949 –)

Ray Magliozzi, along with his brother Tom, are best known as "Click and Clack, The Tappet Brothers," hosts of the long-running NPR radio program *Car Talk*. Ray is a graduate of MIT, taught science, and along with his brother opened a car repair shop called The Good News Garage. They made several guest appearances on NPR radio programs in Boston before beginning the highly successful *Car Talk*, which won a Peabody Award in 1992. The brothers also appeared as the owners of Rust-eze in the 2006 Pixar film *Cars* and in a 2008 animated PBS series, *Click and Clack's As the Wrench Turns*.

Naomi Sims (March 30, 1948 – August 1, 2009)

Naomi Sims is considered the first African-American supermodel, and in 1986 became the first African-American model to appear on the cover of *Ladies' Home Journal*.

Kenneth Welsh (March 30, 1942 –)

Canadian-American actor Kenneth Welsh is known for his role as villain Windom Earle in the television series *Twin Peaks* and as the father of Katherine Hepburn in the 2004 film *The Aviator*.

Warren Beatty (March 30, 1937 –)

Warren Beatty has been nominated for 15 Academy
Awards as an actor, producer, screenwriter, and
director, winning Best Director for 1981's *Reds* (in
which he also starred) and the Irving G. Thalberg
Award. Of 16 Golden Globe nominations, he won six.
Beatty is one of only two people (along with Orson
Welles) to have been nominated for best producer,
director, writer, and actor in the same film, for *Reds*
and the 1978 film *Heaven Can Wait*.

Warren Beatty

John Astin (March 30, 1930 –)

John Astin is best known for his eccentric comedy characters, most notably Gomez Addams in *The Addams Family*. He was married to actress Patty Duke from 1972 to 1985.

John Astin (left) as Gomez Addams and Carolyn Jones (right) as Morticia Addams from *The Addams Family*

Richard Dysart (March 30, 1929 –)

American actor Richard Dysart is best known for his Emmy-winning role as Leland McKenzie on the TV series *L. A. Law*, and has appeared in such films as *Being There*, *The Day of the Locust*, *Mask*, and *The Hindenberg*.

Peter Marshall (March 30, 1926 –)

Peter Marshall (Ralph Pierre LaCock) is best known as the original host of the game show *The Hollywood Squares* from 1966 to 1981, and has appeared in a number of television and film roles, including a cameo in the 1982 film *Annie*. He was inducted into the American TV Game Show Hall of Fame in 2007. He took his stage name from his home town college, Marshall University.

Turhan Bey (March 30, 1922 – September 30, 2012)

Austrian-born actor Turhan Bey appeared in numerous Hollywood films including *Raiders of the Desert*, *Ali Baba and the Forty Thieves*, *Follow the Boys*, and others, becoming known as the "Turkish Delight" to his fans. He worked in Europe as a photographer and stage director, and in the 1990s guest-starred in various television series including *SeaQuest DSV*; *Murder, She Wrote*; and *Babylon 5*.

Turhan Bey

Public Figures

Piers Morgan (March 30, 1965 –)

British journalist Piers Morgan is known to American audiences as the host of *Piers Morgan Live* on CNN. He also appeared as a judge on *America's Got Talent* and *Britain's Got Talent,* won *The Celebrity Apprentice,* and wrote for several British tabloids.

Charles Lightoller (March 30, 1874 – December 8, 1952)

Charles Lightoller was the most senior officer to survive the sinking of *RMS Titanic,* and was a key figure in the inquiries following the disaster, though he later recanted much of his testimony, which had been designed to keep blame away from the British Board of Trade and the White Star Line.

His recommendations for improvements in maritime safety, such as mandatory lifeboat drills and minimum lifeboat capacity, became widely adopted. Lightoller was later decorated for gallantry for his World War I naval service, and in retirement sailed as a volunteer in the evacuation of Dunkirk.

Science and Technology

Sergey Ilyushin (March 30 [O.S. March 18]*, 1894 – August 31, 1945)

Soviet aircraft designer Sergey Ilyushin (Сергей Ильюшин) founded the Ilyushin aircraft design bureau, which designed World War II aircraft including the Ilyushin Il-2 fighter and the Il-4 bomber.

Following the war, Ilyushin developed commercial airliners including the Il-18 turboprop and the Il-62 jet, both of which saw widespread international use. (*O.S.: See pg. 74)

Stefan Banach (March 30, 1892 – August 31, 1945)

Considered one of the foremost mathematicians of the 20th century, Stefan Banach helped create modern functional analysis theory, and is credited with numerous mathematical concepts named for him, including Banach spaces, Banach algebras, and the Banach fixed-point theorem.

Mary Whiton Calkins (March 30, 1863 – February 26, 1930)

American psychologist Mary Whiton Calkins was the first woman elected president of the American Psychological Association.

Although she completed her Ph.D. requirements at Harvard University and was recommended by all her professors for the degree (William James said she had given "the most brilliant examination for the Ph.D. that we have had at Harvard"), she was denied a degree by the university president on the grounds that she was a woman.

She was offered a degree from Radcliffe, a women's college associated with Harvard, but refused it because she had not earned a degree from that institution.

As a researcher, Calkins developed the paired-associate technique, created a system of self-psychology, and performed pioneering research in dreams and memory. She wrote four books and published over a hundred papers and served on the faculty of Wellesley College.

She is regarded as the first woman to earn a doctoral degree in psychology, although the degree itself was never awarded.

Robert Bunsen (March 30, 1811* – August 16, 1899)

German chemist Robert Bunsen was one of the most admired scientists of his generation. He discovered the elements caesium and rubidium and was one of the pioneers of photochemistry and organoarsenic chemistry. Working with his laboratory assistant Peter Desaga, he developed an improvement on laboratory burners, which became known as the Bunsen burner, still used in laboratories everywhere.

*There is some controversy as to the exact date of Robert Bunsen's birth. While the parish register for his birth as well as two documents written by Bunsen himself cite March 30 as the date of his birth, numerous later sources give the date as March 31. Bunsen Burner Day, celebrating his best-known invention, is observed on March 31.

Robert Bunsen

Sports

Laurie Graham (March 30, 1960 –)

Canadian downhill skier Laurie Graham won six World Cup victories and represented Canada at the 1980, 1984, and 1988 Winter Olympics.

She was inducted into the Canadian Ski Hall of Fame and Canada's Sports Hall of Fame, and received the Order of Canada in 1998.

Jerry Lucas (March 30, 1940 –)

Basketball center and power forward Jerry Lucas was named one of the 50 greatest players in NBA history in 1996, and was selected for Sports Illustrated's five-man College All-Century Team in 1999. He was inducted into the Naismith Memorial Basketball Hall of Fame in 1980. Following his career, Lucas became a well known memory expert.

Willie Galimore (March 30, 1935 – July 27, 1964)

Willie "The Wisp" Galimore was a running back for the Chicago Bears from 1957 to 1963, and played for Florida A&M in college, for which he was elected to the College Football Hall of Fame. A civil rights activist, he helped integrate all-white hotel facilities in his home town of St. Augustine, Florida, and his home there is honored with a Freedom Trail marker.

Words

Tom Sharpe (March 30, 1928 — June 6, 2013)

English novelist Tom Sharpe is known for his *Wilt* series of satirical novels about a frustrated community college lecturer, as well as for the novels *Porterhouse Blues* and *Blott on the Landscape,* both of which were turned into BBC television series.

Seán O'Casey (March 30, 1880 — September 18, 1964)

Irish playwright Sean O'Casey's famous works about the Dublin working classes include *The Shadow of a Gunman* (1923), *Juno and the Paycock* (1924), and *The Plough and the Stars* (1926).

Paul Verlaine (March 30, 1844 — January 8, 1896)

French poet Paul Verlaine was a leading figure in the Symbolist movement, elected as France's "Prince of Poets" in 1894. His famous works include *Clair de lune,* which was set to music by Claude Debussy, and *La bonne chanson,* set to music by Gabriel Fauré. The opening lines of Verlaine's poem "Chanson d'Automne" were used in World War II to signal the French Resistance that D-Day operations were about to begin.

His personal life was turbulent. His affair with poet Arthur Rimbaud (right) ended when Verlaine shot the 18-year old Rimbaud twice, wounding him slightly in his left wrist.

Following his imprisonment for attempted murder, Verlaine lived in England for a number of years, returning to France where he succumbed to drug addiction, alcoholism, and poverty.

Anna Sewell (March 30, 1820 — April 25, 1878)

English novelist Anna Sewell is best known for her only novel, *Black Beauty*, published in 1877. She died five months after its publication, just long enough to see that it was a success. *Black Beauty* has sold over 50 million copies, making it one of the best-selling books of all time.

Un Coin de Table (The Corner of the Table), by Henri Fantin-Latour (1872), Paul Verlaine (seated, left) and Arthur Rimbaud (to his right)

The Dinky Bird (1904), Maxfield Parrish

Who Died on March 30?

Art and Illustration

Maxfield Parrish (July 25, 1870 — March 30, 1966)

American painter Maxfield Parris's art is distinguished by its saturated hues and neo-classical imagery.

Crime and Punishment

Chester Gillette (August 9, 1883 — March 30, 1908)

Chester Gillette was convicted for the highly publicized 1906 murder of Grace Brown and died in the electric chair. Theodore Dreiser based the character Clyde Griffiths in his 1925 novel *An American Tragedy* on Gillette, adapted in the 1931 film of the same name and again as a 1951 Academy Award winning remake, *A Place in the Sun*.

Fashion

Beau Brummell (June 7, 1778 — March 30, 1840)

Beau Brummel was a fashion icon during the Regency period in England. He is credited with introducing and making fashionable the modern men's suit and necktie.

His name became known as a synonym for fashion, and a paint color (Beau Brummel Brown), a hybrid rhododendron, and the British rock band The Beau Brummels are named for him. He is also referenced in the Billy Joel song "It's Still Rock and Roll" with the line "You could really be a Beau Brummel baby, if you just give it half a chance."

BEAV BRVMMEL
a Single hair annoyed him

his custom was to go over his face with a pair of nippers. Hairs that survived the razor were pulled out by the roots.

Brummel was famous for his grooming at a time when good grooming was the exception and defects were covered with patches and paint.

Today in any gathering of business men you will see the freshness of face and ruddiness of skin that is due to the tonic effect of a daily Gillette shave.

Just lather briskly, rub in well: use the Gillette with an angle stroke: dip the face in cool water and pat dry with a soft towel.

A Gillette shave is quick and cool, safe and sanitary. It is velvet-smooth, no matter how wiry the beard or tender the skin. Adjust the handle for a light or a close shave. A keen, fresh blade is always ready. No stropping—no honing. Prices $5 to $50. Blades 50c to $1. the packet. Dealers everywhere.

GILLETTE SAFETY RAZOR CO.
BOSTON, MASS.

THAT greatest dandy of all times, Beau Brummel, set great value on the smoothness of his face. After shaving,

TRADE *Gillette*

KNOWN THE WORLD OVER

No Stropping – No Honing

An 1917 advertisement for Gillette razors featuring Beau Brummell

Journalism

Dith Pran (ឌិត ប្រន) (November 20, 1908 — March 30, 2004)

Cambodian photojournalist Dith Pran survived the Cambodian genocide and was the subject of the 1984 Academy Award-winning film *The Killing Fields.*

Alistair Cooke (November 20, 1908 — March 30, 2004)

Journalist and television personality Alistair Cooke was known for *Letter from America* and *Alistair Cooke's America,* and as the host of the PBS series *Masterpiece Theater* from 1971 to 1992.

Gabriel Heatter (September 11, 1890 — March 30, 1972)

Radio commentator Gabriel Heatter's World War II-era sign-on, "There's good news tonight!" became a popular catchphrase.

DeWitt Wallace (November 12, 1889 — March 30, 1981)

Magazine publisher DeWitt Wallace co-founded *Reader's Digest* magazine.

Music

Phil Ramone (January 5, 1934 — March 30, 2013)

Recording engineer Phil Ramone co-founded A&R Records. He produced music by such artists as Burt Bacharach, The Band, Chicago, Bob Dylan, Aretha Franklin, Billy Joel, Elton John, Quincy Jones, B. B. King, Madonna, Paul McCartney, Liza Minelli, Luciano Pavarotti, Paul Simon, Frank Sinatra, and Stevie Wonder. He also recorded Marilyn Monroe's "Happy Birthday to You" to President John F. Kennedy.

Performing Arts

Michael Jeter (August 26, 1952 — March 30, 2003)

Tony- and Emmy-winning actor Michael Jeter played Herman Stiles on the sitcom *Evening Shade*, and appeared in such films as *Zelig*, *The Green Mile*, and *The Polar Express*.

James Cagney (July 17, 1899 — March 30, 1986)

American actor and dancer James Cagney is considered one of the greatest actors in American cinema. Originally known for gangster roles in such films as *The Public Enemy* and *Angels With Dirty Faces*, he won an Oscar for playing George M. Cohan in *Yankee Doodle Dandy*.

James Cagney

Bobby Driscoll (March 3, 1937 — March 30, 1968)

Child actor Bobby Driscoll starred in Disney films including *Song of the South* and *Treasure Island,* and served as the animation model and voice for the title role in *Peter Pan*. He received an Academy Juvenile Award in 1950. He died in poverty after a prison term for drug abuse.

Public Figures

Jaime Escalante (December 31, 1930 — March 30, 2010)

Bolivian-American educator Jaime Escalante taught calculus at Garfield High School in East Los Angeles from 1974 to 1991. He was the subject of the 1988 film *Stand and Deliver,* portrayed by Edward James Olmos.

Queen Elizabeth the Queen Mother (August 4, 1900 — March 30, 2002)

Elizabeth Bowes-Lyon became Queen Consort of the United Kingdom when her husband George VI ascended the throne in 1936. On the death of George VI, her daughter Elizabeth became Queen Regnant, and she became known as the Queen Mother. A highly popular member of the royal family, she was active in public life until a few months before her death at the age of 101.

Portrait of Her Majesty Queen Elizabeth the Queen Mother,
by Richard Stone

Douglas Douglas-Hamilton (February 3, 1903 — March 30, 1973)

Air Commodore Douglas, Douglas-Hamilton, Duke of Hamilton and Brandon, was a pioneering aviator who piloted the first flight over Mount Everest.

Sports

Bob Turley (September 19, 1930 — March 30, 2013)

"Bullet Bob" Turley had a baseball career that spanned from 1951 to 1963, winning the Cy Young Award, the World Series Most Valuable Player Award, and the Hickok Belt. Following his baseball career, he co-founded the company that would become Primerica Financial Services.

Red Hickey (February 14, 1917 — March 30, 2006)

As head coach of the San Francisco 49ers, Red Hickey created the "shotgun formation" in 1960.

Words

Daniel Hoffman (April 3, 1923 — March 30, 2013)

Daniel Hoffman was the 22nd Poet Laureate Consultant in Poetry to the Library of Congress.

Jean Toomer (December 26, 1894 — March 30, 1967)

Harlem Renaissance novelist and poet Jean Toomer is best known for his 1923 book *Cane*. His grandfather, P. B. S. Pinchback, was the first person of African-American descent to become governor of a US state.

März (March), by Hans Thoma

The Month of March

"Up from the sea, the wild north wind is blowing
Under the sky's gray arch;
Smiling I watch the shaken elm boughs, knowing
It is the wind of March."

— *"March," John Greenleaf Whittier*

In ancient Rome, March was the first month of the year. As the first month of spring, in the Mediterranean climate it marked the beginning of the military campaign season. That's why March (Martius) is named in honor of Mars, the Roman god of war.

Although the first month of the year was moved back to January sometime during the transition of Rome from a kingdom to a republic (historians differ), March was the first month of the year in Russia until the end of the 15th Century, and is the first month of the year in many other cultures and religions.

In the northern hemisphere, March 1 marks the beginning of meteorological spring. In the southern hemisphere, March is the equivalent of September, making southern hemisphere March the beginning of autumn.

March is one of the seven months that have 31 days in it. March starts on the same day of the week as November every year, and except for leap years starts on the same day as February. March starts on the same day of the week as the previous June except for leap years, and in leap years starts on the same day as the previous September and December.

March in Other Cultures

The month of March has different names in different languages. Some nations use calendars other than the Gregorian, and their months may overlap with November. Still, they often have a word for November itself.

Arabic (Egypt, Sudan, Yemen): مارس (Māris)

Chinese and Japanese: 三月

Croatian: Ožujak

Czech: Březen

Finnish: Maaliskuu (earthy month).

Greek: Μάρτιος

Hebrew: מרץ

Hindi: मार्च

Korean: 3 월에 (3 wol-e)

Old English: Hreþmōnaþ

Polish: Marzec

Russian: март

Slovene: Sušec

Ukrainian: березень (birch tree)

Vietnamese: 腋呬 (tháng ba)

March Superstitions

"Beware the Ides of March (March 15)!"

"March comes in like a lion and goes out like a lamb."

"April borrowed from March three days, and they were ill."

The first three days of March are unlucky "blind days." If rain falls on these days, farmers will have poor harvests.

Children born on Easter Day will be fortunate; children born on Good Friday are doomed to be unlucky.

"If Our Lord falls in Our Lady's lap / England will meet with a great mishap." (If Good Friday or Easter fall on Lady Day, March 25, the Feast of the Annunciation of Our Lady, national misfortune will befall.)

Clothes washed on Good Friday will never come clean.

Children should not climb trees on Good Friday.

Bread baked on Good Friday will never go moldy; eggs laid on Good Friday will no spoil.

Marriages that take place during Lent will have trouble.

"Married when March winds shrill and roar / Your home will be on a distant shore."

Good days to be married in March are March 3, 5, 13, 20, and 23. Which day? "Monday for wealth, Tuesday for health, Wednesday the best day of all, Thursday for losses, Friday for crosses, Saturday for no luck at all."

March Symbols

Birthstone Aquamarine and bloodstone, both representing courage.

Aquamarine

Birth Flowers Daffodils

Daffodil

March Events

Honorary Months

Presidents, Congresses, and nations around the world issue proclamations recognizing particular months to honor certain causes. These events generally fall in March. (All US unless otherwise noted.)

- American Red Cross Month
- Child Life Month
- Fire Prevention Month (The Philippines)
- Irish-American Heritage Month
- Colorectal Cancer Awareness Month
- National Caffeine Awareness Month
- National Celery Month
- National Cheerleading Safety Month
- National Flour Month
- National Frozen Food Month
- National Noodle Month
- National Nutrition Month
- National Peanut Month
- National Sauce Month
- Women's History Month (celebrated in Canada during October)

Women's Suffrage Demonstration 1917

"March Madness" (United States)

The NCAA Men's Division I Basketball Championship, popularly known as "March Madness" or the "Big Dance," is a single-elimination tournament to establish the champion college basketball team.

Moveable and Multi-Day Events

Some events take place over a specific week or time period. Start and finish dates may vary from year to year. Some events occur on different days each year (such as "fourth Saturday of a month").

Birkat Hachama (ברכת החמה) (Judaism)

According to the Talmud, the Sun was created at the vernal equinox position at the beginning of the

Jewish month of Nisan, established by tradition as March 25 on the Julian calendar.

The Birkat Hachama, "Blessing of the Sun" is recited when the vernal equinox occurs at sundown on a Tuesday, which happens every 28 years. When the Julian calendar gave way to the Gregorian calendar in 1582, the date shifted forward, and continues to shift slowly forward by approximately a day per century.

Birkat Hachama took place on April 8, 2009 (14 Nisan 5769), and will occur next on April 8, 2037 (23 Nisan 5797).

Birkat Hachama at the Western Wall, 2009

Earth Hour (International)

On Earth Hour, held on the last Saturday of March each year, households and business are urged to turn off all non-essential lights for one hour between 8:30pm to 9:30pm on each person's local time. The goal is to raise awareness of the need to take action on climate change.

Meat-Free Week (Australia)

Meat-Free Week, the last week in March, promotes vegetarianism.

National Cleaning Week (US)

National Cleaning Week, the last week of March, reminds us to start our spring cleaning.

Pediatric Nurse Practitioner Week (US)

Pediatric Nurse Practitioner Week is celebrated during the last week of March.

Seward's Day (Alaska)

Seward's Day, celebrated on the last Monday in March, commemorates the signing of the Alaska Purchase Treaty on March 30, 1867.

Easter Season

La crucifixion by El Greco

The Christian holiday of Easter in Western
Christianity is held on the first Sunday after the
Paschal Full Moon following the March equinox,
which is officially set at March 21 by church
reckoning. Easter itself can therefore occur as early
as March 22 and as late as April 25, but occurs most
often in April. In Eastern Christianity, which uses the
Julian calendar, Easter occurs between April 4 and
May 8. This also sets the date for the various events
that lead up to Easter, most importantly the events of
Holy Week.

Passion Sunday

The fifth Sunday of the Christian season of Lent is
known as Passion Sunday in various Protestant
denominations and by some traditionalist Catholics.
Sometimes, the sixth Sunday of Lent is referred to as
Passion Sunday, but it is more commonly known as
Palm Sunday. Passion Sunday starts the two-week
Passiontide, which ends on Holy Saturday, the day
before Easter, commemorating the day that Jesus's
body was laid in the tomb. The fifth Sunday of Lent
can occur as early as March 8 (though the next time it
will be that early is in 2285 CE), and as late as April
11.

Palm Sunday

The moveable feast of Palm Sunday commemorates
the triumphant entry of Jesus into Jerusalem, an
event mentioned in all four gospels. In many
Christian churches, palm leaves are distributed to the

worshippers. The earliest date for Palm Sunday is March 15, and the latest is April 18.

Maundy Thursday

The Thursday before Easter is Maundy Thursday, when the Last Supper took place. Because of its relation to Easter, the earliest day it can occur is March 19, and the latest it can occur is April 22.

Good Friday

Good Friday, observed during Holy Week on the Friday preceding Easter Sunday, commemorates the crucifixion of Jesus and his death at Calvary. Because of its relation to Easter, the earliest day it can occur is March 20, and the latest it can occur is April 23.

Holy Saturday

Sometimes called Easter Eve or Black Saturday, Holy Saturday commemorates the day in which Jesus's body lay in the tomb. Some mistakenly refer to this day as "Easter Saturday," but that properly describes the Saturday following Easter, the last day of Easter Week. The earliest it can occur is March 21, and the latest it can occur is April 24.

Easter

Easter celebrates the resurrection of Jesus Christ on the third day after his crucifixion. In the liturgical calendar, Easter follows the season of Lent, and begins the period known as Eastertide, which ends on Pentecost Sunday.

Easter is observed religiously in a morning service. In the U.S., it's also common to decorate Easter eggs and make Easter baskets of eggs and candy, often with the Easter bunny as a symbol. The White House traditionally hosts an egg hunt, and many communities have Easter parades.

Easter customs around the world include bonfires (Cyprus, western Sweden), men spanking women with a ceremonial whip (Czech Republic and Slovakia), egg fighting (Bulgaria), cross-country skiing and reading murder mysteries (Norway), and children dressed as witches collecting candy door-to-door (other Nordic countries).

Easter Eggs

Easter Monday

In some Roman Catholic and Eastern Orthodox cultures, the Monday after Easter is celebrated as a holiday. It is also known as Egg Nyte, featuring egg rolling competitions and dousing other people with water that had been blessed with holy water the previous day at mass. Easter Monday is also celebrated as Family Day in South Africa. In Guyana, people fly kites that were made on Holy Saturday. In Portugal, it is known as the Anjo (Ivy) Festival, in which people picnic in the countryside.

Śmigus-Dyngus (Poland, Hungary, Czech Republic, Slovakia)

The Monday after Easter in Poland and in the Polish diaspora is known as Śmigus-Dyngus, or simply Dyngus Day in the US. Boys throw water over girls they like and spank them with pussy willows. Girls avoid getting wet by giving boys "ransoms" of painted eggs.

Easter Week (Western Christianity), Bright Week (Eastern Christianity)

The period from Easter Sunday to the following Saturday is known as Easter Week. In both Western and Eastern Christianity (where it's known as Bright Week), the resurrection continues to be celebrated in church services. Easter Tuesday is a public holiday in the Australian state of Tasmania.

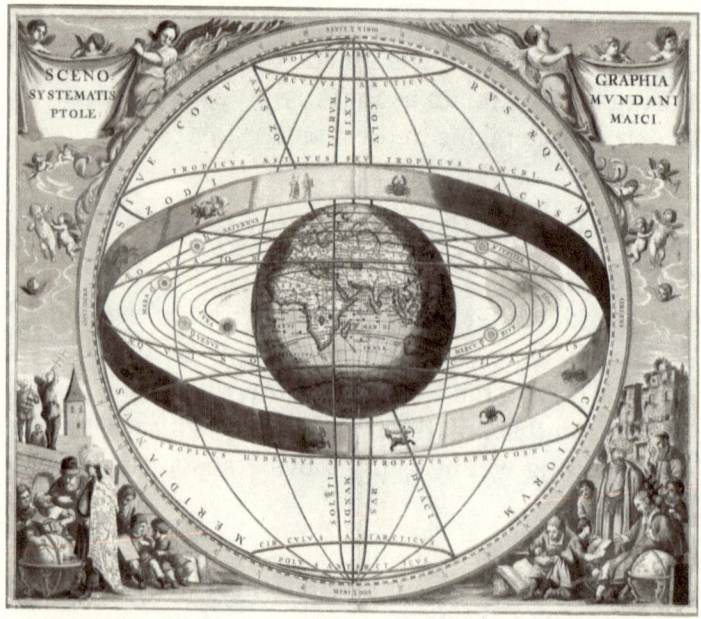

Scenography of the Ptolemaic Cosmography, by Johannes van Loon, based on Andreas Cellarius's *Harmonia Macrocosmica,* 1660

March Zodiac Signs

From the perspective of someone on Earth, the Sun appears to move through the sky throughout the year, along a path astronomers call the *ecliptic plane*. The ecliptic plane is divided into twelve constellations, known as the zodiac, based on traditionally observed patterns of stars. On your birthday, you can't see your constellation, because it's in the daytime sky.

The zodiac was first developed by Babylonian astronomers about 2,500 years ago. Because they were unaware that the Earth wobbles like a spinning top (known as *precession*), they didn't make allowance for the fact that the Sun's path through the zodiac changes over time.

That means there are now two sets of dates for your birth sign. The *tropical dates* are the original Babylonian dates; the *sidereal dates* tell you where the Sun actually appears as it moves along its annual path.

For March 29, the tropical sign is **Aries**, and the sidereal sign is **Pisces**.

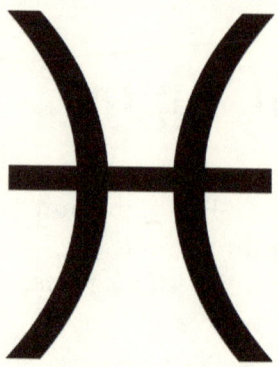

Pisces

Tropical February 20 to March 20
Sidereal March 15 to April 14

In the Roman legend of Venus and her son Cupid, they escaped the clutches of Typhon, known as the "father of all monsters," by transforming into fish and tying themselves together with rope. That's why the name Pisces is plural for fish. The constellation appears as a somewhat ragged "V" shape, representing the rope, with the "fish" located at the two rope ends.

In astrology, Pisces is a water sign, compatible with the other water signs Cancer and Scorpio, as well as with the earth signs Taurus, Virgo, and Capricorn. Pisceans are supposed to be imaginative, compassionate, unworldly, secretive, and escapist.

Aries

Tropical March 21 to April 19
Sidereal April 15 to May 15

In Greek mythology, Aries is a ram with golden wings and golden wool who rescued the twins Phrixus and Helle from certain death. Although Helle died in the rescue attempt, the grateful Phrixus sacrificed the ram to Zeus. The golden fleece from the sacrificed ram played a prominent part in the later myth of Jason and the Argonauts.

In astrology, Aries, a fire sign, is compatible with the other fire signs of Gemini, Leo, and Sagittarius, and to a lesser extent with air signs Scorpio and Libra. Arians are supposed to be adventurous, enthusiastic, quick-tempered, and impulsive.

Illustration by Edward Penfield

What Day of the Week is March 30?

On what day of the week does March 30 fall?

Surprisingly, this isn't an easy question. Because the calendar year is 365 days long (366 in leap years), it doesn't divide evenly by the seven days of the week.

Also, the Earth goes around the Sun in about 365-1/4 days, so a calendar tends to drift over time. That's why the same date falls on different weekdays in different years.

This is made even more complicated by a change in calendars that took place in 1582. Our modern calendar has its roots in ancient Rome, in a calendar reform conducted by Julius Caesar. Caesar commissioned mathematicians to attack the problem, and they came up with the idea of leap years, and thus standardized the calendar for centuries to come. This was called the Julian calendar.

Over time, however, the small errors in Caesar's calculation compounded. That's why Pope Gregory XIII commissioned the Gregorian calendar, used in most of the world today. Some countries converted in 1582, when the calendar was first developed; some converted later; other still haven't changed.

Gregorian and Julian aren't the only types of calendars. The Hebrew year, the Islamic year, and many other calendars are used in different parts of the world and among different people.

You can convert Gregorian dates to other calendars, including the Hebrew calendar, the Islamic calendar, and even the Mayan calendar by visiting the Fourmilab Calendar Converter at http://www.fourmilab.ch/documents/calendar/.

Chinese calendar systems are quite complex and have changed several times; a full discussion is far beyond the scope of this book. If you're interested, you can find information here: http://www.hermetic.ch/cal_stud/chinese_cal.htm.

On Names and Dates

Historians use "CE" (Common Era) and "BCE" (Before the Common Era) instead of the more common "AD" (Anno Domini, or Year of Our Lord) and "BC" (Before Christ), reflecting the fact that the year-numbering system established by the Gregorian calendar is used throughout the world in many countries not culturally Christian.

The CE/BCE designation dates back to at least 1708, and has been adopted as a standard by the United Nations and the Universal Postal Union. Because this series of books covers events and people of all nations and cultures, we use the CE/BCE terms.

The abbreviation "O.S." ("Old Style") on some dates refers to the fact that the Russian Empire did not switch from the Julian to the Gregorian calendar at the same time as the rest of Europe, and therefore some figures and events have two dates.

Also, in the Julian calendar in England in the 16th century, the year began on March 25 rather than January 1. To avoid confusion with Gregorian dates, dates between January and March were often written using both years.

People and events whose original names are not in the Western alphabet have their native names (where possible) in the appropriate script shown in parenthesis. If you are using an e-reader to access an electronic version of this book, all characters don't always display on all devices.

A 50-year brass perpetual calendar.

Cartoon by John T. McCutcheon

Copyright, Credit, and Contact

Follow Us

Our blog Dobson's Improbable History (http://improbhistory.blogspot.com) features short articles on events and people associated with each day, and updates several times each week. You can also get a daily "What Happened In History" message and all the latest Timespinner Press news by following us on Facebook at https://www.facebook.com/TimespinnerPress. Our Twitter feed @SidewiseThinker links you to all our News of the Day.

Contact Us

Find an error or a format problem? Want information about the series, about us, or about when the volume for your special day might be available? Please email us at editor@timespinnerpress.com. (We also take requests if your special day isn't yet complete. Please give us at least six weeks' notice if possible.)

Sources

We owe a great debt to Wikipedia, which is our first stop for research. We attempt to make independent confirmation of all important dates and facts through a variety of other sources. Other sources we frequently use include the Library of Congress; "on this day" listings from *Encyclopedia Britannica*, the *New York Times*, and the BBC; *Chase's Calendar of Events*; and, of course, the always essential Google.

All art and photographs are either in the public domain, used under a Creative Commons license, or with a "fair use" justification, and most frequently come from Wikimedia Commons and the Library of Congress Prints and Photographs Division.

Attribution is provided where possible, or as requested by the copyright owner, or when there is particular historical significance, listed below. For information about any particular illustration or photograph, please contact us.

Credits

- The cover image is a portion of the 1889 painting Irises by Vincent Van Gogh, and is in the public domain because its copyright has expired. The original can be seen in the Getty Center, Los Angeles, California.

- The illustration of the month of March used on the back cover and as the frontispiece is from the French Gothic illuminated manuscript *Les Très Riches Heures du duc de Berry* by the Limbourg Brothers, Jean Colombe, and an intermediate painter whose name is lost to history.

- The 1964 drawing of playwright Seán O'Casey was done by Reginald V. Gray for *The New York Times*. It was released into the public domain by the artist.

- The 1889 self-portrait of Vincent Van Gogh is in the public domain because its copyright has expired. The photograph is part of The Yorck Project Gesellschaft für Bildarchivierung GmbH and is from the DVD entitled "10.000 Meisterwerke der Malere." While it is our position that a photograph of a public domain image is itself in the public domain, The Yorck Project has licensed the images under the GFDL.

- Vincent Van Gogh's 1885 *De Aaarappleters (The Potato Eaters)* is in the public domain because its copyright is expired. The original is in the Van Gogh Museum, Amsterdam.

- *The Starry Night (De Sterrennacht)* was painted by Vincent Van Gogh in 1889. It is in the public domain because its copyright is expired. The painting is in the collection of the Museum of Modern Art, New York.

- The photograph of US President Ronald Reagan shortly before the assassination attempt is in the public domain as a work created by the US federal government.

- The engraving of Dr. Crawford Long is in the public domain because its copyright has expired.

- The copy of the Alaska Purchase check is in the public domain as a work created by the US federal government.

- The 1910 photograph of the Queensboro Bridge (then called the Blackwell's Island Bridge), comes from the Detroit Publishing Co. collection, donated to the Library of Congress in 1949. According to the library, there are no restrictions on the publication of this photograph.

- The photograph of the immediate aftermath of the attempted assassination of Ronald Reagan is in the public domain as a work created by the US federal government.

- The 1815 painting *Self-portrait at 69 Years* by Francisco Goya is in the public domain because its copyright has expired. The original is in the collection of the Royal Academy of Fine Arts of San Fernando, Madrid.

- *Mehmed II entering Constantinople* is by the Italian painter Fausto Zonaro (September 18, 1854 — July 19, 1929). It is in the public domain because its copyright has expired.

- The photograph of Tracy Chapman at the 2009 Cactus Festival in Bruges, Belgium, was taken by Hans Hillewaert and is used here under CC-BY-SA 3.0. The image has been cropped and adjusted for its use here.

- The 2009 photograph of Eric Clapton was taken by F. Antolín Hernandez, and is used here under CC-BY-SA 2.0.

- The 1975 publicity photograph of Warren Beatty from *Shampoo* is in the public domain because it was published in the United States between 1923 and 1977 without a copyright notice.

- The 1964 publicity photograph of John Astin and Carolyn Jones as Gomez and Morticia Addams in *The Addams Family* is in the public domain because it was published in the United States between 1923 and 1977 without a copyright notice.

- The publicity photograph of Turhan Bey is in the public domain because it was published in the United States between 1923 and 1977 without a copyright notice. The photograph has been cropped and enhanced for its use here.

- The engraving of Robert Bunsen is by C. H. Jeens, and is believed to be in the public domain according to the US National Library of Medicine.

- The 1872 painting *Un Coin de Table (The Corner of the Table)* by Henri Fantin-Latour is in the public domain because its copyright has expired. The original is in the Musée d'Orsay, Paris. The photograph used here is part of The Yorck Project Gesellschaft für Bildarchivierung GmbH and is from the DVD entitled "10.000 Meisterwerke der Malere." While it is our position that a photograph of a public domain image is itself in the public domain, The Yorck Project has licensed the images under the GFDL.

- The 1904 Maxfield Parrish painting *The Dinky Bird* is in the public domain because its copyright has expired.

- The 1917 Gillette advertisement is in the public domain because its copyright has expired.

- The publicity photograph of James Cagney is in the public domain because it was published in the United States between 1923 and 1977 without a copyright notice.

- The 1986 portrait of Queen Elizabeth the Queen Mother by Richard Stone was placed in the public domain by the artist under CC0 1.0.

- The painting *März (March)* is from the calendar book Festkalender by Hans Thoma. It is in the pubic domain because its copyright has expired.

- The photograph of aquamarine has been released into the public domain.

- The photograph of daffodils is by "Myrabella," and is licensed under CC-BY-SA 3.0.

- The 1917 Women's Suffrage demonstration comes from the Library of Congress, Prints and Photographs Division, LC-USZ62-31799 DLC, and is in the public domain because its copyright has expired.

- The 2009 photograph of Birkat Hachama at the Western Wall is by "Ingo," and is used here under CC-BY-SA 3.0.

- The painting *La Crucifixión* by El Greco is located in the Museo del Prado. It is in the public domain because its copyright has expired.

- The photograph of Czechoslovakian Easter eggs was taken by Jan Kameníček, who has released the image into the public domain.

- The painting *März*, from the Flemish *Brevarium Grimani*, is by Gerard Horenbout and Alexander and Simon Bening. It was first published around 1510. It is in the public domain because its copyright has expired. The original is in the Biblioteca Marciana.

- The 1906 automobile calendar is by Edward Penfield, and is in the collection of the Library of Congress Prints and Photographs Division. It is in the public domain because its copyright has expired.

- The 50-year perpetual calendar photograph is in the public domain.

- The cartoon by John T. McCutcheon is from his 1905 collection *The Mysterious Stranger and Other Cartoons by John T. McCutcheon*. It is in the public domain because its copyright has expired.

License Description and Terms

Aside from material purely in the public domain, photographs and other material in this book are used under specific licenses permitting free use, usually with an attribution requirement. For full text and terms of these licenses, click or enter the appropriate links below. If you believe there is an error in the copyright status or attribution of any of these images, please email us.

- Creative Commons Attribution 2.0 Generic (CC-BY 2.0): http://creativecommons.org/licenses/by/2.0/deed.en
- Creative Commons Attribution-Share Alike 3.0 Generic (CC-BY-SA 3.0): http://creativecommons.org/licenses/by-sa/3.0/

Michael Dobson

Timespinner
Press